The book of
Divine
Messages

365 words of Wisdom and Guidance

By

Amelia Bert

DON'T MISS THIS BEST-SELLER BOOK.

IT WILL CHANGE YOUR LIFE.

In this book, the Angels respond to all your inquiries, thoughts and prayers. They share their wisdom, enlighten and empower. There are lessons to be learned, benefits to be gained, assistance to be given, truth to be revealed.

They talk to you directly, if you would only allow the words to move through you, you will succeed your own personal transformation.

This book is a direct Angel narration by intuitive Amelia Bert. It is the result of her spiritual journey of months of meditation and connection with lighted spirits.

This spiritual book links all the pieces together, by revealing the truth of the cosmos.

GET IT NOW IN ALL ONLINE BOOKSTORES!

And on this website: http://ameliabert.com/

Amelia Bert

<u>*PREFACE*</u>

I know the importance of daily support and guidance. Especially from a source that is so wise, honest and pure, that can help you shift your whole life around. I consider myself extremely blessed to have such guidance by my side anytime I need it. A few years ago I crafted my intuitive skill, and I succeeded in connecting with my Higher Self, and then the Angels themselves. Now I have excessive support, from spirit guides, spiritual masters, and many other wise beings anytime I need it.

I have to admit, once I had succeeded such interaction I spent hours every night talking to them, about my life, my path, about the world and how everything truly works. (If you want to know more about all that, I will shamelessly direct you to my book "The Truth of All that Is" that is direct channeling from them.) However, as with anything, we get too caught up in our daily lives to have time for that anymore, but anytime something comes up, and I need guidance or direction I can easily tune into their energy, and I get their powerful and wise guidance. I wish all of you had this gift up your sleeve because it is empowering and it brings the needed strength in a difficult phase of your life or assistance to make the right decisions in life. With that in mind, I have collected 365 Messages from Them, and I bring them to you in this small book. I am serious, I have asked Angels, Spirit Guides, my Higher Self, Spiritual Masters to speak words of wisdom to you, to bring direction and support when you need it the most. They eagerly came forth and so we co-created this book full of goodness and divine energy.

It is easy to use, fun and most of all, helpful. Read the following chapter to get an idea on how to use it to get the best message at the right time.

I hope I have succeeded my quest to assist you in those moments you need a little direction. May this book be your companion in good times and in bad.

Thank you for reading.

<u>Introduction</u>

It is no shame to need some help and direction here and then. That is why we love our mothers so much, and our friends, they help and guidance. Now this book brings you an even better companion in such moments; The Angels, Spirit Guides and Spiritual Masters. This book is created to bring Angelic wisdom, inspiration, and guidance on a daily basis, or any time that it is needed.

The messages are guidance from the Angels, Ascended Masters, and Spiritual Beings to help us cope with our everyday life, bring support and Divine Energy. As each message pass on from the Ether, none is written randomly. They guide you to the correct message, at the right time you need it. If you are in need for some instant guidance, clear your mind and think of your question. Then flip through the pages and stop in one randomly. The clearer your state of mind, the more direct the guidance you will receive from them through this book.

Another way to use this book is to read a message before you start your day. There are 365 Divine quotes for everyday guidance. If it is some guidance on what to do that day, it will ensure it helps you, or if it is words of wisdom, have them in the back of your mind as you go about your day. You may need them a few hours later.

Apart from the written message, take a look at the number as it might help answer your question or give you an indirect guidance. Your subconscious helps you understand those messages. Similar to an Angel card spread or even Tarot reading, this book gives guided and direct answers to your questions. The key is to have a clear state of mind and a direct question in mind.

Get the free Ebook on transcribing Angel Numbers to have a better understanding of the numbers showed. You can find it for free here: http://amzn.to/29kbVGt

I hope you find guidance from the Divine Messages, wisdom, and peace of mind.

<u>*MESSAGE* 1</u>

You are unlimited, Divine, powerful and pure.

MESSAGE 2

People make mistakes. It's why you were sent to earth to experience and learn, so you have your free will to choose your friends, job, desires and decisions. You are allowed to make mistakes. When you do, you have the option to make them right, to not re-do them. Forgiveness is not made for those who repent, but for those who have been hurt. You make a choice as well to free your soul from their mistakes than carry them around with you. They might have repented, but if you hold it against them, you carry their burden.

MESSAGE 3

Do not look back, the past is gone, and it only exists in memories. If you don't recall it, it no longer is. Every minute is a new opportunity to start again and direct positive energy into your each moment. Use the gift of time well.

MESSAGE 4

You are not a physical being that has a spirit, but a spirit that has a physical body. There is not an end to the journey of the soul.

MESSAGE 5

When you talk to us, we hear you, we respond. Stay still in silence, and you will feel us there.

MESSAGE 6

We want you to have more fun, find some time for only you. Restore your faith in your abilities and be in love with all you are. Because we do love all you are, and all you have achieved. You may not think it's enough, but they are enough for now. Bravo to all you are, we love you so, never stop believing in yourself and your capabilities. You can conquer worlds.

We love you so.

MESSAGE 7

Life is not a burden but a chance to learn, experience, shine and have fun. Enjoy all the moments with a smile and see the good in every occasion. We know sometimes you get thrown down, but you get up again stronger and wiser. We offer you a hand at those difficult times, and we promise you the sky will clear and you will see the sunshine.

MESSAGE 8

Do not look upon the darkness, sadness, and misery, turn away from all that so that you only see the light, kindness, and bliss. By turning away you are protecting yourself from all those negative emotions and frequency, you are doing a gift to yourself by remaining pure and happy. It Is not insensitive to ignore what will bring you down, to move passed people who will cause you sadness, but it is treasuring yourself first.

MESSAGE 9

Recently you have been feeling lost, confused. You seek for answers, and as you cannot find them, you feel more sad and frustrated. It is to remind you that you are far from lost, allow this time to pass you by and trust that is only the crossing of a bridge, as you cross it, the answers will be revealed. You are not standing alone but moving forward, even if you cannot see this yet, we see how far you have come. The path will soon be revealed.

MESSAGE 10

Do not stop hoping for something better. Do not settle for what does not fulfill you. Why do you think there is not something better for you? Why do you believe you don't deserve anything more? You are wrong; you exist to have, to be, to get all that make you happy. If there is anything less than that, it is not right, because you see and you deserve EVERYTHING that you desire. Remove that old pattern and replace your thoughts with new ones that capture the greatness of all that you are.

MESSAGE 11

Your family is where you should turn to for support, courage, and empowerment. Their love is so great that as you tune into it, you can face anything that comes your way. Whenever you feel alone, lost, confused, or sad, they will bring you back up. You are much stronger this way, acknowledge that source of energetic power, and you can tame anything.

MESSAGE 12

Many dear souls resemble Earth as a playground. They see it a chance to have fun, play and learn. When you enter the physical body, you forget this, and you worry, fear and get discouraged. We remind you that life is but a playground, and you are there to enjoy it. Do not needlessly worry and overwork and stress, but have fun along the way. We love you so very much

MESSAGE 13

The key to a happy state of mind relies on your emotions in the present.

MESSAGE 14

Insight is all you need to make this decision. You know what the answer is already, but you don't want to face it. Staying still, however, will not solve what you feel, will not change your situation. The only way is for you to act. Do it with determination and knowing that it is for the better. And so it is.

MESSAGE 15

Enlighten those around you, smile to those you don't know, wave at the children, feed the animals, water the plants, you spread kindness and love with actions, you receive it from all around.

MESSAGE 16

Don't work for material things; do not struggle to acquire belongings as those are not going to stay. Work for something that helps, that teaches. Create something that will stay and will benefit you and others, that will be remembered, and it will expand you as well.

MESSAGE 17

Do not ponder on yesterday. You are a better person today, and the future will bring you something better if you only allow it. Because of the past you are here now, greater, wiser, appreciate what it brought and now look ahead. Get excited about your future and enjoy the moment. The past does not serve you any longer. In the future, we see new horizons, greater than ever.

MESSAGE 18

Allow your creativity to take the lead. You have so many great ideas, but not enough time to execute them. Inspiration is divinely inspired, they are not random thoughts, but they are helpful tools to help you on your path. Use them, and you will benefit the most.

MESSAGE 19

Life is not about the work left behind; it is about the moments of joy.

MESSAGE 20

Soon you will have to face an important decision. Consider your options wisely and take the time to clear your mind before you commit. We lovingly alert you, so you prepare for such a crossroad. Both decisions will benefit you in different ways. Weight your options and go with what makes you feel better. There is nothing that you HAVE TO do. It is your life, your free will, your decision. Do not worry, whatever you decide it will be the right pathway.

MESSAGE 21

The current path that you have in your mind, the one that keeps wishing for and dreaming about is not far from your reach. You are only a few positive emotions, a few thoughts away towards its greatness. We don't want you to ponder on what is not there, but to what it already is because this is the fastest way to get to that desired outcome. Be happy, be grateful, be expectant, and what you believe, shall conquer what you now see.

MESSAGE 22

We know that you feel that your current job is not fulfilling you. That is not your path. As you struggle and feel drained working there, let it be your sign that you are right. No job should be a struggle, if you don't have passion, then you don't have a goal. And now you are asking us what to do next: do not resign until you find your passion. Then you will be ready to move on. When you find excitement, then follow that path.

<u>*MESSAGE 23*</u>

Let the pain wash away; there are great things waiting for you still, ahead.

MESSAGE 24

If you let go of fear, doubt, and reasoning, you will see with the eyes of the source, feel with pure positive emotions, bask in love and appreciation.

MESSAGE 25

Signs are revealed to you as we and the cosmos communicate with you often, and all you have to do is notice to translate our messages.

MESSAGE 26

Close your eyes. Pause for a minute. Today has been stressful for you, and you need to allow at least this minute to quite your thoughts. Just breath in all around. Hear us talk to you, be with you every minute. We let you know; All is well.

MESSAGE 27

We know you are to receive this message, as it is supposed to reach you. There are no coincidences you see, every matter, every incident, every thought you make matters. And so, you have come this far now. There is nothing in the past anymore, look how far you have come, all the things you have created, why are you saddened by what was. Life is moving forward, not backward and so should you. If you only knew how many more great things lay ahead, you wouldn't miss what's gone, even for a second. Smile, for your future, is so bright.

MESSAGE 28

We hear you asking us what to do next, how to move forward. The roads are open for you, but you do not see beyond what is there now. Spread your wings, aim your targets high and you are going to achieve it. You are unlimited, and you have what it takes to succeed. You know what your next step is; you think of it often. Spread your wings, and aim for the stars. We are going to watch you fly.

MESSAGE 29

Speak your mind; do not go on observing and living passively with another's decisions, this is your time, your life, your choice. It is time to go after what will make YOU happy. The others will follow you, don't follow them but your happiness. We forever support you.

MESSAGE 30

When you see someone who needs help or is sick, do not pity them or think low of them as they are on their own path to greatness. Their hard lessons are important as well. It brings greater growth which helps the soul matures faster. You are living this physical journey for great things, we want you to have only good experiences and enjoy them all, but the bad ones are lessons as well. What makes them pass you by, is the courage, determination, and faith. Never lose those qualities. You are ascending.

MESSAGE 31

We know you are to receive this message, as it is supposed to reach you. There are no coincidences you see, every matter, every incident, every thought you make matters. And so, as you have come this far, there is nothing in the past anymore, look how far you have come, all the things you have created, why are you saddened by what was. Life is moving forward not going back, and so should you. If you only knew how many more great things lay ahead, you wouldn't miss what's gone, even for a second. Smile, for your future, is so bright.

MESSAGE 32

Close your eyes. Pause for a minute. Today has been stressful for you, and you need to allow at least this minute to quite your thoughts. Just breath in all around. Hear us talk to you, for we are with you every minute to let you know; All is well

MESSAGE 33

We bless this body to experience well-being. We treat this soul to be rejuvenated and see only happiness. We form a bond between you and us to charge you in any time of need. This bond links us to restore your energy in body and mind. Not to be afraid. You are linked to us; you are linked to all, you are all.

MESSAGE 34

Opportunities come and go. If you missed one, there would be another. Do not be so hard on yourself as when a door closes, another one opens. Your attitude and desire direct your fate. If you want something, you will get the chance to achieve it. We believe in you, believe in us; your chances are coming.

<u>*MESSAGE* 35</u>

Step away from the crowd. We lovingly nudge you to find some quiet time and contemplate. When too many are involved, it is ten times harder to hear your voice. It is a time to find inner peace to listen to your inner voice. It is alright to ignore your friends or loved ones sometimes because you are the one that really knows your path.

MESSAGE 36

The loss you sometimes face is only temporary. This physical life is given graciously, and once anyone resides in it, continues greater beyond the physical body. No soul is ever lost. Wipe your tears away and smile knowing all is well and will continue to be. Angels of heaven look after you and your loved ones. Never doubt this, but if you want to be reminded simply pray for them. Your prayers are well honored.

MESSAGE 37

We know you are seeking for physical companionship the most. We understand that, and we support it. Humanity is created to leave together and not apart. Some people you find dear might be drifting away, as your energy shifts, your environment does as well and the people that surround it. It is not a negative outcome of your energy but a positive one. As you vibrate in higher frequencies (you are a match for us, and you can receive our messages more) physical beings that are of lower energy – that used to be a match to you before – they are no longer a match. At the same time, you attract higher vibrational people, events, and circumstances. You are in a time of transition, however, as your energy stabilizes you will be able to notice and welcome all the new experiences that wait to happen for you. Do not lose hope; do not think this has been in vain as even though you are not seeing it right now, changes are happening at an energetic level. Bear with it, continue inviting positive energy, and you will soon see all the changes that are about to manifest.

MESSAGE 38

The key to a happy state of mind relies on your emotions in the present.

MESSAGE 39

Bright day makes a happy person or the other way around. You control the world, your experiences, the people who come into your path, even the weather. You could only see what wonderful things you create if you smile and laugh often. A happy mood gives you a happy life. Remember that.

MESSAGE 40

We know you have gone through pain. Pain is temporary. A Loss is an unpleasant emotion, but it has its purpose. Sometimes, angels of heaven assist you to lose something that is not a match for you so that you can find your way to the right one. Whether that is a house, a person, a job or a lover, no loss is ever ad justly. It took place because frequencies did not match anymore. Do not worry about the right ones are well along the way.

MESSAGE 41

As soon as you wake up in the morning, think of something pleasant. Something that will make you smile, even if you force the emotion, or the memory, the energy that is captured stays with you for a long part of the day. We love it when you are happy and blissful.

MESSAGE 42

Close your eyes and breathe slowly. Forget everything that is going on around you right now. Remove those thoughts that interrupt your quiet. Right now is a moment of peace and bliss. You deserve it. Breathe slowly and admire the wholeness of all that you are. What a wonderful person you are, what a glorious figure, how wise and true. Feel the pride feel your lungs. For this is the way, we feel for you. Remind yourself often that you are the king of your own universe.

MESSAGE 43

Divine Timing is not a coincidence; It is God's way of bringing together affairs that are aligned with each other, so there are expansion and lessons for all involved.

MESSAGE 44

So what if you don't have a car or the money in your wallet run low? Belongings and possessions do not measure Life, but with lessons and moments. If you took the time to worry a little less every day and have a bit more fun, you would see that all your problems will gradually disappear. Worry is a negative emotion that does not match your energy, the more you worry, the more the problem persists. We do not kid you with this, as you let it go, you will see the light, you will have a clearer mind to know what to do. Allow yourself to relax and trust that all will take care of itself. In the meantime have some fun and relax. All is well.

MESSAGE 45

Time does not exist where we are. In the physical world, it exists to bring order. Do not worry about the years that have gone by, instead smile for the ones that lie ahead. We will tell you a secret, while in spirit; you can visit them once again. Nothing is ever lost.

MESSAGE 46

Pause and look around. What do you feel? What do you see?

Experience this moment with all your senses, because this moment is as perfect as it can be.

MESSAGE 47

If you have a positive thought or an inspiration associated with uplifting energy, you are aligned with your Higher Self that assures you that thought is positive and beneficial.

MESSAGE 48

Find reasons to be happy. Look around and notice the things that make you smile. Today is the day that beautiful things begin. Make sure you are on board with them.

MESSAGE 49

Money is energy. Let it flow.

Receive and spent in balance.

Give with an open heart, the way you like to receive.

When you give in this way, you make way for the flow of abundance, and so, you will never run out.

<u>*MESSAGE* 50</u>

"What is my next step?" you have been asking us and wondering.

But are you listening? The answers always come if you pay attention.

<u>MESSAGE 51</u>

Lay alert at all times, as any opportunity can come from various resources, and many are in disguise. As you are happy you vibrate positive energy and only great opportunities lie ahead.

MESSAGE 52

As you rely on others for respect, love, and appreciation, you keep yourself in the corner. Value your opinion, ideas; respect and love all that you are; YOU are the most important person in the world!

MESSAGE 53

Close your eyes and breathe. Right this moment, we reside within your being. We are

there, sending you positive vibrations. Feel them, sense them, bask in them. We open doors for you; we make way for many beautiful things to enter your experience.

MESSAGE 54

Whenever there is a dis-faction of your physical body, it is created by negative thoughts and emotions, your physical body then translates that to stress, worry, sadness, negative thinking, all these may result in the response of your body functioning in alignment with those thoughts. There is truly a great power in your thoughts.

MESSAGE 55

What if I told you today, something wonderful is about to happen; what would be your response? do you believe that today is an amazing day? Believe it and watch it transform. Today you attract positive experiences!

MESSAGE 56

In many instances, there are those who do not agree with you, those that have opposite ideas and perceptions. If all were created the same, then all will make the same decisions and live the same lives. There is beauty in the creation of each one. If you could see past your differences, you will find the peace and excitement of having different goals and ideas. No one is born alike, yet we are all made of the same pureness and light. Learn from others and accept their choices, they are evolving and so are you.

MESSAGE 57

If anyone has created what you wish to receive, then why do you think it is difficult or impossible for you? All of you are created equally and equally deserve the abundance of the universe. Begin to feel that power runs through you because it is the only way to attract it. You are powerful, can you feel it?

MESSAGE 58

You have come this far, you have grown, you gained all those experiences. You have become wiser. Do not look how far you are away from your aspirations, but look how far you have come to be that wonderful person you are now. It is alright; you don't have to have everything now, to be all that you ever wanted to be today. It is the beautiful experience of the journey. You are moving towards that now. You are always moving ahead, if you take a look back, you will see that indeed, you have walked miles. What would you do if all you ever wanted to be and do was here now? What would you be moving towards then? You will get there; believe that you are always moving towards better things. Enjoy the journey; there is a wonderful year ahead. We are so proud of you.

MESSAGE 59

You can't jump that high. You must first love where you are NOW. If you only focus on where you want to go, you are saying that you don't like where you are. If you don't love your present moment, the next one will only be one of the same.

MESSAGE 60

Change the way you see a problem, and then it will change too.

MESSAGE 61

Everything comes to you at the right moment. Trust that in divine timing, when you are most ready, you will receive and then you will know why you haven't received before.

MESSAGE 62

Tomorrow is a new day; don't keep playing the same one. What was, was.

MESSAGE 63

If you ask us for assistance, in any matter as that would be, we will guide you towards a smoother resolution. We will open up pathways. We will bring you signs. When you ask us for help, we always respond, but you must seek for our responses as they come in many ways. Follow our synchronicities, trust your intuition and you will be guided, you will notice our reply. We always respond.

MESSAGE 64

As you grow older in age, you change, evolve, and become wiser and better. As a result, people, events, and circumstances that used to be a match for you are no longer so they must fall away so that new ones take their place. It is like the tree that changes leaves; you are changing too.

MESSAGE 65

To uncover the rest of who you really are, love all that you are.

MESSAGE 66

At this point do not hold yourself back, be open to new opportunities and possibilities and do not rely on a few people to make you feel worthy. You are becoming bigger than them now. You are the one that will make yourself important and happy if you only continue trying.

MESSAGE 67

Once you find your passion, be driven by it, find the excitement for something new, something you like, something you want may this be all the sign you need. Why do you limit yourself from anything you desire? Are you not important to have what pleases you? We don't see it that way. We and the universe are ready to assist you whenever a new desire is born within you to help you bring it to life. If you continue being excited and passionate about it will come to life. Like a young child wanting a new toy. The child likes the idea of the new toy. It becomes a passion for getting it. It imagines all the great fun it will have with it. The child doesn't care how or when it will get that toy; it is only driven by the desire and passion towards it. And then the whole universe works to fulfill that passion.

Do not deny your wishes, do not overshadow them either but embrace them, do not ponder on how impossible it is to have it but make the decision to get it no matter what, and then wait for the right opportunity.

MESSAGE 68

Deep within, lies the power of all knowledge. Yes, you do know all there is to know even though you do not remember them all at first. The more connected you are to your higher self, the more feedback you acquire regarding how the universe is and works. What if one told you "You are all that you can see" Do you believe that? Ponder upon the words quietly, do not judge, do not think, just listen. Listen to the feeling that comes to the surface, is it excitement, knowing or is it a tightening? There you will know the truth.

MESSAGE 69

For others to love, accept and honor you, you must love, accept and honor yourself. The others pick up on the frequency you emit. You do not need anyone else to accept you, find acceptance within.

MESSAGE 70

We want to bring messages to those who read now. You came forth into this journey to experience all that this life will bring. If you focus on beauty then so you will see it if you focus on misery, then that is all you see. You create your paths; you make the decisions. Whatever they are you learn from them; You grow, whatever path you are and wherever you are going you can choose another. We urge you to stand a while and think of your path until now. Is it pleasing you? Are you happy with you are, the experiences you have gained and the people that surround you? Make this moment count the most. After this you will know whether to keep going or start another path, it is never too late. If you do not like something, change it. We support your choices and your journeys. We help to bring you clarity. Pause NOW. We bring you peace.

MESSAGE 71

You rush into your daily lives, and you do not pause to breath, to notice what is happening around. There is so much beauty that waits for you to notice. Nature is created for all to see and be admired. People appear in your life to share and gain new experiences. Events and signs keep repeating for you to pause and realize their messages. But you rush and the minutes to hours become months and years, rarely pausing to see how far you have come. There is power in the present moment for those who appreciate it. Stop only for a second and notice all that is happening, where you are, experience this moment with all your senses. It is how you ground yourself, appreciate and love and grow. We love you anyway.

MESSAGE 72

People come and go from your life for a reason. You meet the right person, the right time to help you move on, offer you guidance help, or inspiration. Perhaps they become friends for life, maybe they pass through, but their presence is enough to move you on a new journey. Spirit guides connect us all together when they know we can benefit the most. Those that leave from your life, they are not a match any longer, you outgrew them, they hold you down. Their moving away is but you rising higher.

MESSAGE 73

We love and surround you, always. Find us within in a feeling, feel our touch in a breeze. See our signs in patterns. We are around.

MESSAGE 74

The rest of the world doesn't matter.

You are the whole universe.

MESSAGE 75

Today read the following words out loud and feel their energy.

"I allow the universal energy of good fortunes of health, vitality, prosperity, and love to shower upon me, to move through my ethereal body; through my affairs, my occupation, my home, and my loved ones. Strengthen them all and fill them with that which they lack to be good, strong and healthy. Thank you for all that which I now have, thank you for all that which I am. I recognize that I am part of the universal energy, and I deserve the flow of good vibrations through my physical experience. Thank you for letting me experience it, now I allow it to fill me."

MESSAGE 76

Nothing is too big for you, for you are an exception of God and all your wishes will be provided. Do not be afraid to ask.

Do not hesitate to dream.

You can have it all.

MESSAGE 77

Love all that you are, notice your achievements. Stand in front of the mirror and congratulate yourself. Acknowledge where you have been and how far you have come now. You need some boost of confidence from yourself. And then you will begin to feel more connected. Then you will receive direct guidance, inspiration, assistance.

MESSAGE 78

It is your views about the food you consume that is fattening and not the food itself.

Eat guilt free, bless your food, enjoy its taste and learn to love yourself. It all starts from within.

MESSAGE 79

You must acknowledge wishes to bring miracles into your life, to materialize what you hold in thought, and to allow the universe to bring them to you.

MESSAGE 80

Go with the flow. Do not over think, stress or worry. In this way, you become the perfect match to your desires.

MESSAGE 81

Relax, and you will see the answer, you will see the safe boat that we send to rescue you out of this situation, and there is not only one; there are plenty that will keep coming to you until you are safe and sound.

There are opportunities; there are safety nets, people, and resources. Do not lose your faith, hang on and help is on the way. We promise you. Allow yourself to see; relax help is on its way.

<u>MESSAGE 82</u>

You are never alone, you may not see us there, but you have begun to feel our presence with you. We try to nudge you and bring you inspiriting messages. Sometimes you pick them up. We want you to know that we are there, even if not in the same physical world, our presence never leaves your side. Whenever you need a close friend, talk to us for we listen to you and we respond if you learn to recognize our signs.

MESSAGE 83

Do not doubt yourself. You are what you are, all that is perfect. We adore you unconditionally, and we have been with you since the start. Your soul has gone through rapid growth, and we want to give you peace of mind. Where you are now, at this moment, is perfect. Acknowledge this, and then where the path will take you next, is even better.

MESSAGE 84

Whenever you feel alone, call for Us.

We never leave you while on a physical journey. Your Guardian Angel and guide oversee you. Call and talk to them, they will shower you with strength, guidance, support and love.

MESSAGE 85

Spent time playing with children or pets. Appreciate being in their presence. In this way, you invite their positive energy to match your own. Be a child once again, run free, play and laugh.

MESSAGE 86

Being in nature restores your energy and brings you upliftment. Be around water, flowers or trees and sense the difference in your energy field. Nature boosts you.

MESSAGE 87

Do not hold back from the things you want. They want you too.

Close your eyes and touch them, sense them, smell them. Have them before they are there. Invite them to join you.

MESSAGE 88

Energy from the environment may be negative as ideas and frequencies of others affect your well-being. Do not hesitate to be excused when you feel drained or overwhelmed. Your energies are the one that matters the most.

MESSAGE 89

The path to where you want to go is a road created by you. By giving your focused attention to the ending result and feeling, you draw it closer. All you have to do is trust that you are guided towards it, let it go, and watch it unfold before your very eyes.

MESSAGE 90

The path unfolds as you walk through it. There is nothing destined because you create your tomorrow with your now. Wherever you focus your attention NOW, it will be that path that unfolds for you TOMORROW. Caring how you feel at this moment matters more than anything else.

MESSAGE 91

You are special in your own way. You have talents and gifts, you make different choices, and you choose different paths. All of you have strengths, and you are very special and powerful. Even if you don't see it yet, we do. We see your worth, and we know you have so much to give. You are truly perfect.

MESSAGE 92

Evil does not lurk around you. You should not fear it for it only follows those who hold themselves back from Divine gifts, nor feel the love and beauty that is all around. Evil only lurks into the imagination of those who are constantly in low vibrations. It cannot harm you if you are joyful because then, we are all that is around you.

MESSAGE 93

Trust your intuition; you know the answer already, and it will take you whenever you want to go. When it is time, you will know.

MESSAGE 94

The synchronicities that occur are predetermined by the attitude you hold for your desire. If you allow good things to flow when you think about it, more and more synchronicities align for your benefit.

MESSAGE 95

Dream big, there are no boundaries on this universe you stand. Wish for all you need, anything that will make you happy ask for it, and something even better finds their way to you. Asking is the very first step you need to take, everything else just falls into place once you relax and enjoy the moment and go with the flow.

MESSAGE 96

The perfect day unfolds for you as you take the time to appreciate all that is and all that is about to happen early in the day. Choose good feeling thoughts and stay with them. How your day unfolds then, will keep you in awe.

MESSAGE 97

Believe in the expansion of your desires. They are true; they are we are. We see them, feel them. We connect you with them through your emotions, you see. We let you know they are here and we are urging you to get here too. Allow yourself to feel a little bit. Hear us; we are helping you by connecting with your emotions.

MESSAGE 98

Today give something you don't need to another who needs it more. Either that is a gift, food or even service or assistance your kindness is rewarded in many, many more ways.

MESSAGE 99

Your present is the most powerful moment you will ever have.

MESSAGE 100

Do not fear, nor feel anxiety or doubt. Those emotions do not serve you, clear them up, release yourself from them. They block you from your path.

MESSAGE 101

Source adores you and loves to connect with you. Take a few deep breaths and let all your thoughts go. Sit like that for a while and just notice the energy shifting in you. We are connecting.

MESSAGE 102

Everything you want is within your reach. You are here for a reason, and right now, with this message, it is our way to tell you that you're presicely where you should be. You're doing well. Feel happy, praise yourself a little. We are watching you. All is well.

MESSAGE 103

Trust your intuition. Every path that unfolds is a creation of your thoughts and vibrations, and we are always guiding you my physical friends towards the best one. There is an ultimate high connection in you, in all of you. Never feel alone, you never are.

MESSAGE 104

Celebrate your life in any way that you can. Have fun, laugh, cheer, smile, be grateful for all that you have. Say I am grateful now!

Enjoy the moment often, do not care about what you see around, observe what you want. Be a creator of the life you want and cheer every chance along the way.

MESSAGE 105

The ocean sometimes it is stormy, other times it is peaceful. Nature has moments like this as well, one day it is raining, another it is sunny. Changes that happen come naturally to help you experience an abundance of moments.

As you walk down your own path, you might get moments like that, shifts of mood, changes of environment. If everything were still, then you wouldn't grow, you wouldn't gain anything new.

All the moments are of equal glory. Remember this and do not worry when you get a stormy one. The sun always comes up again.

MESSAGE 106

Do not overdo it. Even if something feels good, even if you think it is not harmful, if it becomes a habit, it repeats the same energy. Something that is repeated often becomes stuck energy and does not allow healthy energy to run through. Even if this is something you eat or something you do, your energy needs change and healthy flowing energy.

MESSAGE 107

Time goes by in a flash for us. Whenever you enjoy your time in a physical lifetime, you lose your sense of time passing by. This is because you become a match to your Divine Higher-self, that like Us, has no sense of time. Time is not measured by minutes, but my moments of a good time.

MESSAGE 108

There were times that you felt our guidance directly within. There were times that you knew what the right thing to do is, you had the right answers even if you could not explain it. Sometimes, you even heard it with your own heart and knew it was the wise advice. We look after you, even if you don't see us there, that does not mean that we do not help you out. Have faith, patience, optimism, and you will receive our guidance.

MESSAGE 109

No matter how many times you worry, or obsess about a matter, it won't change unless you change your attitude about it. If you keep seeing it as negative, then it will continue to be, perhaps even attract greater displeasure for you. But if you do not resist, if you do not subscribe to the negative attitude, it will rapidly shift and disappear, or be replaced by something pleasurable. If that is your current job, a person you try to avoid, or even your image in the mirror, if you stop denying it, stop going against it, you will see how well it will fall into place for you.

MESSAGE 110

Sometimes you get overwhelmed with feelings from the Ego. Those "Human emotions" bring you greed, jealousy, displeasure, anger. We understand all those emotions but do not let them consume you. It is not who you are. The nature of all that you are emanates emotions of love, courage, simplicity and kindness.

Remember this next time you get overwhelmed, then just close your eyes and breath clearing your mind from thoughts. Say "I am not my thoughts" and all those negative emotions will turn away.

MESSAGE 111

You did not come here to experience pain, nor displeasure or unhappiness. What you came here for is to live in an abundance of emotions, experiences, lessons and interactions. All is well along your physical path.

MESSAGE 112

Every time you pray, you connect with the higher part of you that is connected to all that is. That higher part of you knows what you need and asks close guides and angels to assist to help you achieve it. Even if you think no-one is listening you are mistaken. Even if you don't pray to anyone, in particular, the right ones are listening.

Pray, and you are always heard.

MESSAGE 113

What you experience now, is only but a small part of all that you are. You come from many years back; you are experiencing only a portion of your physical life right now. Some things that might seem familiar, they might really be, only your soul remembers it and not your memories. A decision, a conversation, a place you might have re-experienced it before, re-lived it. It does not make it any less real for you. Sometimes you return to re-live an event for various reasons. All that you love is never lost. All the people and places are well treasured in memory and energy.

Nothing is ever lost. You live again and again making different choices, taking other paths. Take risks and don't be scared. You probably know the path ahead already.

MESSAGE 114

Before you reincarnated upon this lifetime, you were aware of all that you will face as you embarked upon that physical journey. You were also aware all that you will learn, of all the people you will help with your presence, of all the experiences and lessons you will gain. And you were so thrilled to begin.

Now, don't get discouraged because you cannot remember the reason for your being, trust that where you are has a cause and you are perfect just the way you are.

MESSAGE 115

We know you have felt our presence several times through your life; when you were younger, more frequently than now. Children are purer and can experience our divine essence more than others.

When you are ready to experience our presence again, simply pray. We always come when you call. Close your eyes, and you will know we are there.

MESSAGE 116

Like the stars, you fade as well. All physical living organisms slowly evaporate. This is not to experience loss or pain, but to be re-borne and start again.

The same is with you as you continue your path, for your journey is greater. Nothing is lost. As you start again, you carry with you all the knowledge and lessons, and like this, your soul blooms.

MESSAGE 117

Did you ever consider that the people that are in your life now are not random? They are there to help you grow and expand, to offer you lessons and support. When a person has nothing else to give you, they move away from your life, so that others join you. Let the old go; you outgrew them.

MESSAGE 118

Happiness is your true state of being. Happiness circulates energy in and out of your body, from you and to you. The road to happiness has neither laws nor predestined paths; it is a choice you follow. Notice and count all that you make you happy now, and

appreciate them. Acknowledge something pleasing when it arrives to invite more like it in your life. Love all, act in kindness, spent time with people and activities you love and enjoy; all of those are ways to bring happiness in your present moment and clear away old troubles.

MESSAGE 119

When something is not pleasing you, when you don't have joy in your heart, then it lacks benefits. On the other hand, when something brings you excitement and fulfillment, it matches your inner soul. Only then, wonderful things occur.

MESSAGE 120

Do not believe that something is impossible because we can assure you it is not.

MESSAGE 121

Cry dearest one. Don't let grief into your heart. As you allow tears to run through you, you allow sadness to come out. Then you will feel better, and you can start again, free.

<u>*MESSAGE* 122</u>

Age does not exist in the spirit world. Aging is only temporary for physical beings to experience difference and expansion. As you return to spirit, you will be young once again as your soul never ages.

MESSAGE 123

Look back in your life before and recognize all that which you have learned, all that which you have that you love now, no matter how unimportant they complete your greatness and your lessons.

MESSAGE 124

Singing is sacred. It is an expression of thoughts and emotions. It is the release of tension and sharing happiness. We even enjoy singing. It is a form of celebration. Don't restrain your expression, and sing like no one is watching.

MESSAGE 125

You were wondering how you would know your path, how would you know what you were supposed to do. The truth is, you have clues all you're over your physical life, to help you find your path. Urges, advice, thoughts that come to your mind, other people's inspiration, knowing. We don't leave you undirected. You have grant support, but you also have choices and paths to follow. When you find something that pleases you deeply, then be sure it is the right one for you.

MESSAGE 126

Your physical body is responding to your thoughts with similar energy. If you do not value yourself enough, that might give you negative body responses such us fatigue or loss of temper. As you love and treat yourself kindly your body responds with good health, energy, and vitality.

MESSAGE 127

Someone who sees energy can notice black energy around you when you are sad or worry or afraid. If you needlessly worry this dark energy follows you constantly and enters your physical body. It creates exhaustion, loss of appetite, loss of creativity, frustration and lastly sickness. To remove this dark energy from your energy field fill your life with laughter, fun and positive thoughts.

MESSAGE 128

As you relax and ease into life, you stop worrying and have more fun. Have fun; life should be happy and merry, not filled with thoughts and worry. Let the pain wash away and find your inner peace, happiness. This is how you will be free, exhilarated, happier. Pause regularly and breath, appreciate how far you have come, and be proud of what you have achieved.

MESSAGE 129

Before you close your eyes every night, say thank you to all that made you happy during the day. As you do this, you allow the great things to flow in your life the next day.

MESSAGE 130

Children are free, pure and their natural state is being happy. They laugh constantly, and when they are upset, they experience a great shift of emotion that is confusing and differs greatly from what they are used to. This is the reason they cry often. They dislike the feeling of not being in pure joy.

On the contrary, adults bottle inside their displeasure, and it doesn't seem such a big the leap from happiness.

MESSAGE 131

Enjoy the moment; notice what happens around you, as this will ground you in the present. Relax and smell the flowers, appreciate all sounds, count your blessings, love where you stand.

MESSAGE 132

Give yourself a gift because you deserve it, go on a holiday because you have done so well all these years, appreciate the joy of a nice meal or dessert. Do things that make you feel good and do them more. Get a massage to rest your body, sleep until late if you enjoy it savor your every moment as that is will help you build up desire and enthusiasm and give strength to your body. As you treat your body well, so it will respond. Similarly, if you enjoy good moments, then more of those will come and then some more and some more and will bring you the change that you desire. As energy follows energy, your attitude is the key. You have to start from where you are, and in only so little all will change for the better.

MESSAGE 133

Fight anxiety as it is not a healthy emotion. Every time you feel you get anxious, close your eyes and imagine a bar meter hitting red, breath in and out slowly and watch with your mind's eye the bar meter coming lower and lower and it hits green which means relaxed.

The anxiety will have gone down along with the bar.

We love you and help you anytime you need.

MESSAGE 134

Undoubtedly, we support your decisions, even if they are not of your best interest; they always bring something positive along with them. So next time you make a decision, we encourage you to first thing of what you want to accomplish and do not look for the best one. All of them are best ones for you at this time. This is the reason you were presented with them.

MESSAGE 135

Sit your eyes closed or fixed at one place and think of your day to come. Imagine how you will like to see it unravel. Do this every morning as soon as you wake up for best chance to see them occurring. The universe always receives the frequency of your thoughts, and then it matches it right back to you. Use the power of thought for you, and not against you.

MESSAGE 136

Dream a little success for you. Dreams are only thoughts with desire, and the universe brings your thoughts to manifestation. Think of what you use to dream when you were little; did you get them yet?

MESSAGE 137

Nothing bad is going to happen unless you attract it with your thoughts. Do not endure negative thoughts in your life because you always deserve to have highest of vibration. Anyone, you receive a low feeling thought, replace it with a good one.

MESSAGE 138

Remove hate from your life. It is intoxicating all of your thoughts, emotions and other parts of your life. Hating is not harming another, only yourself.

MESSAGE 139

Pay attention to how you harm others with your words and choices and remember the beauty of all that exists. It is only right to bring happiness and assistance to others the way we assist you. All of you are angels on earth. Help the world, spread joy, be kind. The universe will applaud you.

MESSAGE 140

Be excited for today. What great things will the universe bring you? Think about what would make you happy today, what would you like to experience? Imagine them before you start your day. The universe will deliver, if not the same events, the same frequency, and emotion within you.

MESSAGE 141

Control your thoughts; your focus directs the events that take place. Similar to a remote control that changes the channels. Change the frequency with the shift of your emotions.

MESSAGE 142

Smile at us right now. Smile at the universe. Breathe in Divine Energy and happiness. Experience the pleasure of being alive at this moment, feel it with all your senses. This moment is perfect, and so are you.

MESSAGE 143

You came forth willingly to experience human form and receive all that this life gives you. Your journey here is not to struggle, but to live and enjoy. Your main purpose is to follow your heart and enrich it with human experiences, of enjoying all that it gives. You are not to worry about things that you did not succeed because that is not your journey.

MESSAGE 144

How can one be free of insecurities and troubles?

They see themselves as perfect, and they don't see any troubles only lessons and opportunities.

MESSAGE 145

Find something fun to do today; something that you enjoy, but you never make time for it.

Fix your schedule and allow yourself to enjoy a fun activity because you deserve it. Life is more fun that way.

MESSAGE 146

Do not get distracted from other peoples' opinions. They are free to judge and criticize, but you are the one who holds the strings. This is your life, your choices, your lessons, don't let them overshadow them.

MESSAGE 147

Sleep exists to help your mind and body relax. As you have thoughts dancing all the time, sleep helps to release you from tension, stress and rejuvenate you. Having a balanced sleep is important in your life as it helps to put your thoughts in order, and receive guidance. We join you regularly in your dreams, even if you don't remember.

MESSAGE 148

Don't take life too seriously. It's not the only one!

Have fun, play, experience, breathe and re-evaluate. Set your goals and live your dreams. This is what we encourage you to do.

MESSAGE 149

Today we have a new task for you. Put your responsibilities on hold, and give time yourself. Relax, play, do something that you really love to do. Today it is very important don't let it pass.

MESSAGE 150

Similar to an overworked machine, your mind needs constant breaks. Every hour allow one or two minutes to remove all thought and just breathe. This will allow your brain to function with more focus, clarity, have better judgment and follow our inspiration easily.

MESSAGE 151

You have been focusing on a matter for a while now; we know you are concerned. What will be, will be, and worrying about it will only make it worse. Trust that everything will be resolved for the greatest and highest good of all. Even if you don't know what that highest good is, we do.

MESSAGE 152

You have so many responsibilities; too many people rely on you to make it right, to be there, to do what they expect you to do. This is making you stress out, and overwork your mind and body. You have not come into this life to serve others. You have come to put yourself first, and help others when they need. If another takes advantage of your kindness, it is okay to say "no." Even if that is your children, your boss, co-workers or friends, saying "No" is the break you need to restore your physical and mental condition. It is a requirement every so often, and you need it.

MESSAGE 153

The sun shares energy with earth and all who reside in it. It is there to revitalize, and energize. Standing in the sunlight too long overcharges you while avoiding its warmth weakens you.

Stand under the sun 2 minutes every hour gives you the energy you need. Whenever you feel drained, out of focus or weak, have a little walk outside. A little sun every day is a gift you can give yourself.

MESSAGE 154

Be kind to all, the way you want them to be kind to you. Even if someone is rude, don't repeat their mistakes. Acting in a polite and kind manner equals sharing and receiving with an open heart.

MESSAGE 155

You are not here randomly. You came willingly in this family, in this body, in this life, but you are free to create it the way you want it.

MESSAGE 156

Do not see the lack of money in your life. Remember when you had more, and appreciate anything that saves you money or brings you more than you already have, no matter how small. As you tune into abundance and disregard lack, plenty is all you see and receive.

MESSAGE 157

Wondering what if, what would have been different makes you not living this path you are in at the fullest. You cannot change those past choices, but you can alter the ones you are given. Live with no regrets as the road you are in now, has made you the person you are today.

MESSAGE 158

Do not ponder upon what would have been. You are here now; you made it, you have succeeded in our eyes. Do not look back; stay focused on the now, that matters the most.

MESSAGE 159

Some People have been incarnated along with you to help you gain valuable lessons. Some you know already, others are still to join you. These lessons are important, and they are what you need to expand. They make up in the form of lessons, or negative behavior but all of them serve their cause. If you went through a traumatic experience with someone, it might have been what you needed to expand.

MESSAGE 160

You evolve every day, with every decision you make. You are not who you were a year ago. When you shift, you gain a new perspective, and you become wiser. Value all that you are and all those memories, all those decisions that made you the wise person you are now.

MESSAGE 161

You cannot control all circumstances and events that happen every second. What you can do is change the frequency of your thoughts and attitude, so the right ones match your own.

Change the frequency, into positivity, kindness, and joy. Then all the other events will be under control.

MESSAGE 162

Are you ready to feel our presence next to you?

Then close your eyes and focus on your breath. When you have removed all thought, say out loud: "My loving Angels of the light join me in this room at this moment. I call for you to help me experience your Divine Strength and presence. Thank you, so be it."

Stay still, observe, notice, feel. We surround you.

MESSAGE 163

Today notice what we bring. Experience all that this life has to offer. Just for today do not worry, complain or stress. Just for today, say thank you to nature for all that you enjoy. Appreciate your life, your greatness. Smile at people you don't know, say thank you and mean it. Just for today, we ask that you let go of the ego side and live by the soul.

MESSAGE 164

Pick a color you like. Just for today, every time you see that color pause and observe until you find something that pleases you. Once you find it, appreciate it just for a few moments, then go about your day, and notice until that color comes up again.

MESSAGE 165

Every time a negative thought comes up, reassure yourself that all is working for the greatest good of all.

MESSAGE 166

Your loved ones that have crossed over are not lost, and they have not forgotten about you. They regularly pause their progression to join you in the physical. They may be close to you for days or just a minute, but they make sure to let you know they are alright and help you in any way they can.

They might send you a person for advice, a friend when you are in need. They might even shower you with healing when you need it.

MESSAGE 167

The great ones that like you incarnated to learn and teach. They have achieved their purpose, they have learned from their incarnations, and they have expanded which now are closer to their true existence. You too will join them soon.

MESSAGE 168

Who said pleasure is a sin? All the beauty that exists it is there to be admired, in nature and people. All physical pleasures are there to be savored as well. Flavors, smells, feeling, and physical desire. These are the greatness of living in the physical, to enjoy all that the body brings.

MESSAGE 169

Meditation is a gift and should not feel like a burden. It is the time of stillness which your ego silences and the soul governs. While in meditation you are reminded of the greatness of your soul, you feel joy, love and gain clarity. It is a time to savor.

MESSAGE 170

All that you don't speak, you ignore to think, you hold inside become fears, blockages, and grudges. Speaking up and thinking them over is a way to release what is bothering you.

MESSAGE 171

What makes you happy? What brings you
excitement makes you anticipate, and once it is
there you feel time passing you by fast? Find any
such activities and engage with them often. Those
are the things your soul loves to do.

MESSAGE 172

We shower you with unlimited abundance. It comes in the form of ideas, opportunities, and people. Like a physical check, you need to cash it to get the money.

Be aware and jump into opportunities that feel right, that make you feel good. They are our check to you.

MESSAGE 173

Brothers and Sisters incarnate together to help each other grow. Same as family members, they are not randomly chosen, but they are part of your inner world. Even difficult relationships help you gain something that you were lacking. If you experienced any such event, look back to it with a clearer mind and think of all that which it taught you.

MESSAGE 174

Never fear death. It is only a short moment that transfers you to the afterlife. During that time you are not alone but protected. If you hurt it is but a second, then we take the pain away and heal your soul from within.

MESSAGE 175

Your present is the most powerful moment you will ever have. Treasure it.

MESSAGE 176

The natural state of the body is health. Health governs the body once it has a joyful mind. When the mind become ill and filled with negative thoughts, the body follows. 90% of physical problems are caused by negative thoughts, stress, anxiety, worry. The happier you are, the healthier you will become.

You wonder what the other 10% is, that is an experience needed to be learned.

MESSAGE 177

Have you thought what will happen if you allow yourself to desire? To wish, with no limits? If you could believe that all your wishes will be met no matter what?

Then you will have no more wishes left.

MESSAGE 178

Some chose to join physical life wealthy. Others prefer when they join poor, only to learn the value of it.

If you were only wealthy all your lives, then you would not learn anything knew. This is true for health, love, kindness, respect and all those that exists only because the other does as well.

MESSAGE 179

Tonight, we wish to speak to you directly. If you want to hear us, when you lie in your bed tonight, ask us to join you.

All that we ask you to do is hear us. We speak from within with thoughts.

MESSAGE 180

Ignore all that which bothers you. All those who bring you negative emotions do not belong to you. DO not give them attention; simply let them pass you by.

Those are the things that your higher self-knows. They are unimportant to you, unnecessary, uninteresting and unhealthy.

MESSAGE 181

Today we ask you to call someone dear to you. Perhaps, someone, you haven't talked to in a long time. Someone that is in your mind often.

The memory of them is vital in your mind still because your path together did not end. There are still more to gain. Call them, and they will feel the same too.

MESSAGE 182

Do not stop dreaming and face reality, but keep dreaming and make a reality.

MESSAGE 183

Sometimes what seems impossible at first, it suddenly gets resolved. Ask us anytime to step in, and we always do.

MESSAGE 184

If something does not bring you joy at heart, it is not worth your while.

MESSAGE 185

If the little bird stays close to its mother in the nest, it would never learn to fly.

Take risks, do not be afraid to fly.

MESSAGE 186

When you feel all the others are against you, they create blockages in your path. If you have clarity about where you are going, remove those blockages and run towards your goal.

MESSAGE 187

There are certain key moments in your life, which bring you lessons and guide your life in a new direction. These moments may include meeting a new person, losing a close loved one, getting a promotion, moving into a new place. Those important key moments exist to guide you closer to your life's purpose. Ponder upon some key events in your life, and perhaps you can find where they try to lead you.

MESSAGE 188

Don't be afraid of change. Change brings expansion.

MESSAGE 189

Enjoy your physical journey, learn, expand and empower your being with positivity and good experiences. Then this journey will be the most beneficial.

MESSAGE 190

For each one of you, there are two Guardian Angels to watch over you, perhaps more. You have spirit souls guiding you and many loved ones that surround you.

MESSAGE 191

You have exceptional power. Believe in yourself, and you will find it within.

MESSAGE 192

You are special in any way you are created, in any form you live, in any thought you have and in any mission you have to follow.

MESSAGE 193

When you allow yourself to have a bit of fun, you let go of negative thoughts and emotions, and then wonderful things unfold.

MESSAGE 194

You exist in this reality to be happy, and that includes fulfilling your desires. Everything that you are, we are; and everything that you came to be we help you to achieve it. Your desires are part of your greatness in this life. Do not hide from them.

MESSAGE 195

You have inner wisdom and power already within. Your soul is connected to all of us and has greater knowledge. Trust your judgment more and do not rely on other people's guidance. You are wiser.

MESSAGE 196

Take more deep breaths and be at the moment more frequently, to expand your energy into pure emotions and thoughts.

MESSAGE 197

Be true to yourself, your preferences, your judgment, your skills and your desires. They make all that you are.

MESSAGE 198

Do not underestimate your judgment, opinions and inner knowledge. You are exceptionally wiser.

MESSAGE 199

Stop procrastinating. By finding excuses to avoid from acting you are preventing yourself from advancing and expanding.

There are no excuses and no reasons. There is only will and power. When you know something is right to do, you are not winning anything from avoiding it. This inner knowing it is your guidance, the excuses are the ego.

MESSAGE 200

The more optimistic you are, the more people, events, and circumstances of high frequency match you.

MESSAGE 201

Today do something good for someone else. Kindness is a pure act with powerful energy. You not only help another, but you allow the universe to help you.

MESSAGE 202

Believe that you can, and you will.

MESSAGE 203

Your higher self and we try to assist you to find your path and happiness. We sometimes bring you suspicions because you must really acknowledge if you are happy. We remind you always to put yourself first. Review where you stand and consider: Are you happy? Are you fulfilled? Is this what you really want?

MESSAGE 204

You are abundant in spirit. All that which you seek, are created within your life experience as long as you believe in your power. Once you do believe, you will see how powerful you truly are and all that which you can so easily create. Like God, you hold gifts as well.

MESSAGE 205

Wishful thinking is an abundant way of living.

MESSAGE 206

Wishes are a way of loving your life and wanting to improve it.

MESSAGE 207

Before you begin something new, take a deep breath first; clear your mind and state: *"This is going to turn out beautifully."*

And so it will.

MESSAGE 208

Love your present moment more than the next.

MESSAGE 209

Bless those around you; spread positivity and uplifting energy. As you focus on giving blessings to others, you invite more to join you.

MESSAGE 210

 You worry about money but are they enough to buy happiness? However, happiness does bring money since you tune into the universal energy that shares and gives the same way it receives.

MESSAGE 211

You are at the right time, the right moment, the right place in this place called the universe.

MESSAGE 212

The happier you are, the more blessings you bring into your life.

MESSAGE 213

Are you ready to experience Divine Guidance today?

Choose something we would like guidance with. Perhaps an area in your life that you want to improve, or a question that you need to answer.

Ask the help of your guides and Angels to reveal it to you today.

"I direct my attention to my spirit guides and guardian Angels and ask them to step in today and direct me towards <u>this area of my life</u>/ <u>towards the resolution of this event,</u> and help me acknowledge and understand all that I can do to resolve it and

make it better for the highest and greatest good of myself, and all involved. Thank you, so be it."

Today, know you are guided. Just be aware of the response.

MESSAGE 214

Do not worry or stress or wonder how or when or if, but know you are on the right path.

MESSAGE 215

Trust your intuition; you know the answer already, and it will take you whenever you want to go. When it is time, you will know.

MESSAGE 216

You stress about the future, and you forget the present. Do not strive for a better tomorrow; strive for a good right now.

MESSAGE 217

Friendship is about giving and receiving. People who come to your path join willingly to help you advance and receive in the same way. Relationships that have nothing to offer, often tend to fade and vanish. This is so others can take their places that bring greater benefit. It is similar to a tree that changes old leaves. It is a natural consequence but necessary nonetheless.

MESSAGE 218

Open your windows and let the sunlight come in.
Stand under the sun and ask that it dissolves any
darkness, illness or sadness.

MESSAGE 219

Understand and clear away any negative emotions that you feel, as those are holding you back from expansion. Your soul is wise enough to move forward, do not ponder on what was but what it will be.

MESSAGE 220

Anger is a human emotion. It overflows when in combination with the ego self. Overcome it by finding your peace within. Many will ask us how to do that.

You find it in every kind act, every laughter, and every emotion of love. As you fill your life with those emotions, anger and ego have no part in you any longer.

MESSAGE 221

When you dream, you do not see with your eyes, but with your third mental eye that is awakened and not blocked when you are asleep.

MESSAGE 222

Your Higher Self guides you.

Listen.

MESSAGE 223

Those you have lost are never in fact lost. They wait for you patiently and while they continue their own expansion. They are in peace, joy, and harmony and you shall meet them again.

MESSAGE 224

Patience, you are getting there. Just enjoy the trip and know that you will arrive soon to your desired accomplishment.

MESSAGE 225

Part of your life's purpose is knowledge and understanding. Knowledge of all that you are, and an understanding of the mistakes, so you do not repeat them again. Like a child, you learn and grow.

MESSAGE 226

You have innate talents that are ready to be revealed. Let go of thought and let those skills guide you.

MESSAGE 227

There is always a way to know if something is for your

highest good. Step away from the crowd, be with your thoughts

and ask for clarity; you will know. Your Higher Self guides you.

Listen.

MESSAGE 228

We love you, bless you, and wish you to have a joyful day. Today will be an amazing one!

MESSAGE 229

Today allow us to shield you with protective light, so the world's cruelty does not affect you. Today ask us to step in and empower you, shower you with bright light to soothe and empower. Today, you stand strong.

MESSAGE 230

Stand in front of the mirror and talk to your reflection. That part of you that is connected to the universal knowledge knows all the answers. Discuss what is bothering and don't be surprised with the responses that you come up with.

Talking alone sometimes is healthy, you organize your thoughts, your clear your mind, you set priorities, and you find answers and guidance.

MESSAGE 231

Loving yourself is a crucial step to creating your life. Respect and love your being as you are, recognize your exceptional power, love what you do. The place you stand now is a starting point to glorious experiences that follow.

MESSAGE 232

Like a painting, it begins with a blank canvas. Your life begins and allows you to fill the empty canvas in any way you choose. If you add beautiful colors and drawings, it brightens, if you color darkness and ugly drawings, so the same painting alters its beauty. You are the painter and choose to fill your life's canvas accordingly with beautiful or negative experiences. Your attention is your brush.

MESSAGE 233

Do not merge into another person's life, do not be involved with their drama, negative energy or problems. All you can do is give advice and a comforting ear, but do not get affected by their energy. Know that this is their path and they will learn to deal with it. If you become involved more than you should, you will invite similar results into your own life.

MESSAGE 234

Are you ready to receive direct guidance?

Close your eyes, relax and ask what you would like. Then remove chatter from your mind and listen to the next thought that forms within. It is your Divine-self guiding you.

MESSAGE 235

Sometimes what you came in this life to learn cannot be learned the easy way. There are times that you have to lose someone or something valuable to learn the lesson. Other times, pain comes in the form of experiences and in others sadness to restore some wrong values within. We know you don't like the pain and the loss, but you must understand that nothing is random, even those.

Amelia Bert

MESSAGE 236

Mistakes or wrong doings are rewritten when you learn from them and acknowledge their effect.

MESSAGE 237

Do not concern yourself with another's' choices or mistakes. They live their own path, and they should affect your own judgment and life's path. You may walk side by side with them, but your roads are different.

MESSAGE 238

As you relax your thoughts, as you find a little hope then the sky will clear. Your thoughts are like the dark clouds in the sky that darken it from clearing. As you trust and let go then all those negative clouds will disappear and you will see the light, the sky will be clear once again.

MESSAGE 239

Inspiration, impulses, right place, right time is all how the universe works, how we help, to clear the path and seize your worries.

MESSAGE 240

Money is but the energy that follows thought. If you think of abundance then abundance finds you, if you think of the lack of money then so it shall be. All you have to do is change your attitude and see money in a new light, and so it shall find you.

MESSAGE 241

The pathway to success is not predestined, it is created. All that which you want to have and be is well within your reach.

MESSAGE 242

Bring fresh energy in your work environment, open the windows, let the sunshine to restore energy, arrange the furniture, bring something new, change what you feel to shift the frequency in the space.

MESSAGE 243

Nothing is random. All paths and people in your life help you progress, learn, experience and enrich your physical experience as well your spirit.

MESSAGE 244

You are here for a reason and a purpose. All you have to do is find it.

MESSAGE 245

Patience is a virtue, and if combined with the positive expectation it truly is a gift.

MESSAGE 246

It is never too late to start something new. We see you procrastinate and delay what you wanted to create, even to act on inspiration. Make the time, and you will be greatly rewarded. All you have to is begin.

MESSAGE 247

Mistakes are not wrong; they are only a detour to where you are supposed to be.

MESSAGE 248

Close your eyes and think of an event that would make you happy.

Think that it has already taken place. What have you learned from it? What experiences did you go through? What emotions did it arise?

As you think, you create.

MESSAGE 249

Every night before you go to sleep bless your house, your wallet, the people you love, your health, your work. You bless them by appreciating them and hope that they continue to be good and vigorous.

MESSAGE 250

Plant something in your garden, give life to a plant. This plant then will reward you by beautifying your environment and boosting your energy.

As you give to nature, it gives back to you.

MESSAGE 251

Do not give up. Perhaps at one time, the situation was not a continent, but the next time everything is different, and you might get a totally different outcome.

MESSAGE 252

Practice is all you need to get better. When you set your mind to something, you improve. All you need is will.

MESSAGE 253

Sometimes you need to relax your mind from thoughts. This helps you release old energy and refreshes you with bright new ideas and inspiration.

For this, allow regular breaks through your day for meditation, walks in nature or even napping.

MESSAGE 254

Day-dreaming is a way to relax and raise your vibration.

It brings you positive energy since it associates your desires and brings happy emotions.

MESSAGE 255

TV, news, gossip are forms of misinformation that bring negative energy to your home environment. This is because the news affects your own frequency. Be more careful what you focus on as it controls you.

MESSAGE 256

When you look up at the night sky, appreciate the beauty that exists. All those little stars have their own history and energy. As you stare at them, you connect to their energy. As you do, you cannot but appreciate the whole universe.

This is also true for animals, people, and plants. You are one, but you can connect with all with your focused attention.

MESSAGE 257

Yes, the time is coming for what you have been wanting. Stay positive and release any fears.

MESSAGE 258

Look at the clock. What time does it show? The numbers bring you guidance as well if you only notice more often.

What do the answers bring you ask? Make your own meanings, and then you will know. We help you if you ask.

MESSAGE 259

Sometimes the path you have chosen has multiple destinations. Each one reveals new lessons and brings alternative resolutions. Choose what you want to achieve and let the roads open as you walk along.

MESSAGE 260

Marriage is not about what is right. It is the union of two people wanting to be in each other's lives and making a bond to support, respect, love, and honor. If those values are kept, then the union will be blessed.

MESSAGE 261

You are who you are, and no one can change that. Your preferences, mistakes, and values make the greatness of all you are. Some might want to intervene into your life, others watch ahead and judge, some walk by your side giving support. In any of those instances, you are the one walking the path.

If you ever need guidance and assistance which way to ask for clarity and when your mind is relaxed, you will receive the answer from your own inner guidance.

You will never get lost if you want to be found.

MESSAGE 262

The road to success is not a physical path, but a spiritual one. If you hold positive thoughts and speak words of achievement then, success shall be yours.

MESSAGE 263

The food you consume has energy. Don't weight it in calories but in thoughts that make each portion. Have you given it positive energy before you eat, or did you feel it with guilt and fattening thoughts?

It is not what you eat. It is what you think of it before you eat it.

Try to bless your food and acknowledge its positive elements and so you direct its energy to fulfill that task only. No weight is needed to be added to your body, only good energy.

MESSAGE 264

Forever is a word that has a deeper meaning. Your forever is not until the end of this physical life, but it exists many, many lives ahead and will always continue to be. So when you use that word, remember that it is not anytime soon, and fail to keep your promise.

Words have a frequency, and as that is captured, it is carried along with you, grading you to your promise time and time again.

MESSAGE 265

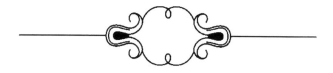

Siblings are not only your physical family but all others as well. Before you hurt another or judge or criticize, know that they might have been your sibling before in another time, and they might be one later.

Treat all with respect and love since we are all part of the same energy, you and us, you and them. We are all siblings coming from the same source energy.

MESSAGE 266

Lies have a deeper frequency that you think. As you speak words, their energy is captured. If you tell a lie, it might not be one for long.

Be careful what you speak of, or even think of and make them only positive ones, like your own personal genie in Aladdin. When you speak and think of it, you rub it with your wish. It does not know what is true or lie, what is indeed needed and what is not. All it knows is energy.

MESSAGE 267

We advise that you start by changing your inner world, make yourself happy first. Once your courage and strength rises, you will see more changes needed to be made to bring you more happiness and joy. From those, a new one will come that will bring you the income and opportunity you were hoping for. Until then work to let go of the sadness so that you can notice the signs.

MESSAGE 268

Do not ignore another's advice. If it comes from your mother, your sibling, a friend or even a stranger, advice is the way we speak to you.

MESSAGE 269

Nothing is over yet. Do not give up on your dreams. You might have taken a long way, but you are getting there if you keep going on

MESSAGE 270

There is not only one lesson here to learn, not only one shift to make. You have faced different pathways; you have given many choices to be where you are now. Hence you have gained many valuable lessons already. The person you are now, with all that which you have created is of endless worth to us, and to you. You are very wise indeed.

MESSAGE 271

Wake up with a smile and a happy expectation. Smile and the universe will give you more reasons to smile. Expect, and you will not be disappointed.

MESSAGE 272

See with the eyes of your soul. Achieve that by seeing with no thought. See with feeling, appreciation, and love. Experience who you really are, removed from ego. This is your true nature, and the more you bring it out, the more you connect with it.

MESSAGE 273

Love your body. The love you give it is captured. It brings health, beauty, strength. The lack of love you give it brings you weak bones, illness, and sadness. Remember to love all that you are and appreciate it completely.

MESSAGE 274

Whenever you worry, or you are anxious, breathe deeply and smile. Say out loud "everything is working out for me, and so it is now."

MESSAGE 275

The start of something new is not always easy. We know this, yet we encourage you to make those big steps because they will bring you new energy, progress, and new experiences. If you only ate the same food every day you would not be fulfilled, change is necessary and beneficial.

MESSAGE 276

You want to know of our confirmation that we are there for you. We are confirming this now in this way, so you know you are not alone. We know you have thought of this at times. Do not wonder any longer. You many not hear us when we respond to you, but you can feel us from within, and that is as much proof as any. Allow us to shine the path for you.

MESSAGE 277

Communication is all that is needed to pass on your emotions and feelings to others. When you hold them inside, you do not allow those emotions to be released and shared. The expression is given to be used and for communication to be established among others. Do not hold it inside; you can speak your mind.

MESSAGE 278

Your pets are in your environment and get affected by your energy. You are also affected by theirs. They do not have egos, and they are in sync with nature and hold high frequency. As you play with them or spent time with them, you tune into their energy and level with your own, and vice versa.

MESSAGE 279

Be more alert on what you are thinking, observing, speaking at any time as it is fundamental for your tomorrow. You hold the key, learn to use it accordingly. The universe always receives what you are sending either with your thoughts, emotions, words or actions.

MESSAGE 280

Thoughts trouble your mind so often that you do not allow new ideas and guidance be given to you. Same as inspiration Divine assistance comes from within. To be able to receive and understand it you must be in high frequency, that is when you are in a good mood, and when your mind is not occupied with thoughts and negative emotions.

To relax your mind and allow fresh energy and guidance daily, we ask that you often pause and just clear those thoughts for a few minutes often.It will also help to elevate you and help you make the right choices.

MESSAGE 281

Do you remember your dreams? As you relax in a deep sleep, your subconscious takes over. It guides you, helps you learn lessons and process what has passed. We can easily connect with you and offer you guidance and support. As those lessons pass directly to your subconscious, you have no memory of them but an unexplainable understanding or knowing.

Call us every night before you fall asleep to enrich you with new lessons and understanding. Even if you don't remember, we will be alongside you.

MESSAGE 282

Nothing is random. Things come together to bring about synchronicities and more ideas and interactions that will contribute to a greater plan for all involved. Do not lose faith but be optimistic and things will fall into place.

MESSAGE 283

The old needs to make way for the new. Do not be sad for the past; do not be afraid of change. All is moving towards a natural flow, and you are moving with them.

MESSAGE 284

The action that is Divinely guided at the right time comes suddenly and is accompanied by strong positive feelings and urge to act, also known as inspiration. Whenever you get this, you should act upon

it; it will bring you positive results.

MESSAGE 285

Nothing is set in stone, as all of you have free will, and opinions to make your own journeys.

MESSAGE 286

Keep a positive attitude that your future will turn out great, and so it will be.

MESSAGE 287

Whenever one believes they are beautiful, others and the cosmos pick up on that frequency and respond accordingly. The same equals with being rich, poor, healthy, abundant and so forth. Make your own beliefs about the world and yourself, and others will follow; the universe will respond.

MESSAGE 288

There are no limitations to the cosmos.

Let the flow of abundance shine upon you.

MESSAGE 289

Today clear your schedule for 20 minutes or more. Dedicate that time to clear your psyche and relax your mind. Remove all thought, emotion, and idea and just be one with your whole existence.

If you succeed, then you will not want to stop.

MESSAGE 290

Anything can be of value, and so do not be so quick to dismiss it. Something someone tells you may even be your next step to take towards your goals and desires or a warning from us. If you dislike that person, you will not receive the message. Give it a chance; maybe someone or something somehow will be that thing you have been waiting for.

MESSAGE 291

Happiness is your true state of being. Happiness circulates energy in and out of your body, from you and to you. The road to happiness has neither laws nor predestined paths; it is a choice you follow.

<u>*MESSAGE* 292</u>

If you are ever in doubt what to do next, take a moment to rest your mind from thought. As you allow time away from the topic, the right thing to do will become clearer for you.

MESSAGE 293

Stand upright with confidence and determination. Your posture shows your attitude, the energy that surrounds your body. With every step remember who you are, what you have achieved, and how great you are. We want others to know because you deserve their respect and awe. You are magnificent.

MESSAGE 294

When you compliment others, the universe compliments you.

When you help others, so you shall find help.

When you think good thoughts, positive changes occur.

When you love yourself, so will others love you.

MESSAGE 295

Let go of the thoughts of how and when and if, it is because universe works in marvelous ways and there is always a great opportunity, chance, a way that the universe brings you what you lust for.

MESSAGE 296

No need to apologize to us for any mistakes you have made. We do not judge you but love you unconditionally. It does not matter if another has forgiven you as long as you forgive yourself. All that matters is to learn from your mistakes and not repeat them again. As you do, those mistakes are immediately deleted.

MESSAGE 297

Do not rely on others for happiness. You are the center of your world and others are only a part of it. Do not make them your castle because you are the king and you rule your world.

MESSAGE 298

Creativity comes once you are relaxed and peaceful. If you want to create a wonderful piece of work, first take some time to be alone with yourself, to relax, to meditate, to feel good about where you stand. As you do just that, your energy raises, and your creativity flows freely.

MESSAGE 299

You do not need to revenge anyone. People's mistakes and wrong actions will follow them, and even if it is in this lifetime or another they will understand the pain they have caused, and they will learn.

Focus on your own path and let others learn from their own.

MESSAGE 300

Notice how animals behave, how free they are, how happy when they are in nature. They do not have egos, but their physical body is well connected with their spiritual one. They achieve this freedom and happiness because they do not have reasoning, right or wrong or any thoughts that trouble them.

You can be more like them by trusting that the universe has your back and you do not need to worry no more. Be a little more like them once in a while. It is your natural way to be.

MESSAGE 301

We know the greatness that is you. We know you can achieve many things only if you set your mind to it. The key to achieving is positive determination. This in combination to all that you are, is a certain victory.

MESSAGE 302

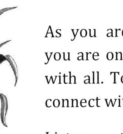

As you are one with your soul, you are one with us. You are one with all. To see this, you need to connect with yourself.

Listen to our guidance. Inspiration strikes when you least expect it. Are you ready to follow it? When you are ready, your guides and higher-self send you signs to get you ready.

We think you are ready now, ready to listen.

Do not ignore your inspiration, your higher-self speaks to you in this way.

MESSAGE 303

We admire your will and strength. You have been strong, and now this is shaking with anxiety. Anytime you worry close your eyes and picture us right next to you. We give you more strength and will need to work through anything in your life. You are very important to us, and we love you unconditionally. There is nothing you cannot face. You have us with you.

MESSAGE 304

What we lovingly ask you to do is to get clear on your intentions. What is it you want to achieve regarding your love life? Find all those aspects that mean the most to you and cherish them in a relationship, friendship or work look for them, and when you notice them, then you will know you are on the right pathway.

MESSAGE 305

Don't doubt your abilities, your choices, your behavior. We ask that you have more faith in you. The greater confidence you have, the more certainty you will have in your life.

MESSAGE 306

There is no need for concerns, God is mighty and so is the abundance of ways and resolutions that will lighten you. As you worry and stress you do not allow yourself to see the light, but you keep yourself at a distance. It make it harder to materialize into your wishes. Let this go and trust that we will sort this matter from now on. Let the burden lift from your shoulders and trust that your angels are by your side and working to resolve this as of your requirements, perhaps to an even better resolution. Do not worry, all is well and taken care of you will be provided for, for you and your family now and in the future. Rest assured.

MESSAGE 307

We would love to see you smile and be joyful. Whatever will come will come, but your state of mind directs the waves of the ocean in other words what you face in life. The happier you are, the stronger you become, the more courage and will you have to go on.

MESSAGE 308

Whenever you need us to boost your self-esteem, call us with a prayer and notice the tingling on your skin. We always come, we embrace, we empower; because that is how strong you are when you have might assistance.

MESSAGE 309

Those who pass on are only taking a break from physical reality. They exist in spirit as no one is ever lost.

Part of their energy exists still in the physical in the form of thoughts you have for them or even objects they wore. However, their soul waits for you in the spirit in a peaceful and harmonious state. All souls return in their state no matter their life lessons, mistakes or kind acts.

Physical life is a time of learning, and once they return to the material world, they learn from their wrong doings, or they are more empowered from the kind acts they have completed before.

MESSAGE 310

Do not let another's judgment bring you down.You have your own power emanating from within and out, coming from other spiritual planes and mighty angels to support YOU. This is how strong you are, and this is how much we believe and support you.

MESSAGE 311

Once you recognize a desire, the journey of it has begun. The ships have sailed, the alignment has been set, the manifestations will not take too long. We just tell you to enjoy the expansion into everything you want to be and want to have.

MESSAGE 312

Harmony is the main factor to a life well lived. Chaos does not allow the soul to thrive.

Make the time to set your affairs in order so that you bring peace and harmony to your daily life.

MESSAGE 313

Not yet. Some actions need to be postponed, not because it will be wrong, but because some of the people involved are not ready for the change. Delay what you had in mind recently and wait for our nudge to act upon it later on.

MESSAGE 314

Children need to feel safe when there is courage they thrive the most. Offer them protection and affection until they are old enough and they will return the favor.

MESSAGE 315

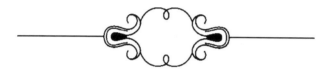

Stop the chatter in your mind. You need peace and harmony to thrive. Go on a walk in nature to restore your energy. Let go of all the worrisome thoughts for today. Rest them for just a day, and then the chatter will dissipate, the answers will rise to solve any worries.

MESSAGE 316

Let love and kindness be your primary emotion and act towards another. As you judge and look down upon others, your own expansion is on hold. As you accept and respect, so you will thrive. Remember what you give out comes back to you.

MESSAGE 317

You come from light, from a powerful source of pure energy and goodness. This part of you exists in quiet, in the pause in between your thoughts. Your thoughts make you human, but you find peace, bliss, divinity in harmony.

MESSAGE 318

Stand straight with your head held high. Whenever you fail you start again, whenever you face troubles they will dissipate. Keep moving on and know that the storm will pass and the sun will shine once again. We know you can do it, we believe in your strength.

MESSAGE 319

You can never fail if you never give up.

MESSAGE 320

Sometimes all that is needed is some time alone. Clear your schedule for an hour, go for a walk, just observe, don't think. Just live, breathe and be.

It is powerful being in stillness.

MESSAGE 321

Something, someone said shouldn't worry you. Something you believe in, however, is what counts the most.

<u>Message 222</u>

It is how you face a matter that makes it a problem or the solution.

MESSAGE 323

You may come from source energy, like all the others, but your own entity is unique, unlike any other. Your way of perception, your thoughts, and your soul are a special combination formed to exist and perceive differently. This is the reason that no one is the same with another, and you are very special in your own ways.

MESSAGE 324

To have a great life, you must pursue your happiness. Without happiness life has no value, and the lessons are not so important.

Happiness lies in your own desires, preferences, and characteristics. Spent more time with yourself to find them have a life worth living.

MESSAGE 325

Eat what is going to make you happy before and after you consume it. That is the key to a great diet.

MESSAGE 326

Do you think of yourself as poor?

If you do, then so you are and will be. But if you consider yourself wealthy, then so will the rest of the world.

MESSAGE 327

The happier you are, the better the life ahead of you.

MESSAGE 328

When you feel low or sad, close your eyes and imagine you are in ahead of time. There you are happy, relaxed and smiling. Be that happy smiling person for a while and then the imagined will be believed.

MESSAGE 329

You are not just one person. You are the whole world.

MESSAGE 330

We know what you are feeling every minute of the day. We translate your emotions, and we are with you when you need us the most. You might hear us whispering you kind thoughts of encouragement, you might feel our energy uplifting yours, or you might see our nudges in nature.

You might not see us, but you can tune into us, the way we can tune into you.

MESSAGE 331

If a pattern keeps on repeating, it is a message. Pay attention.

MESSAGE 332

Complaining will not solve a problem. It will only persist it. To remove something that annoys you, you should not complain about it, but find ways to enjoy it, to appreciate it, then it will vanish.

If you cannot alter the feeling it gives you, then ignore it. It might not disappear, but it will not affect your energy.

MESSAGE 333

Ignorance brings peace of mind. You do not need to know all the details. Sometimes what is in store for you. It has to do with the bigger picture, the final result.

You were born into the physical world to celebrate ignorance; that is why you did not remember anything from before. Ignorance protects you and allows you to move through life free, and we help you find the trails of where you are supposed to go. Do not worry. You might now know what or who or when or how, but we do.

MESSAGE 334

Develop thoughts that make you radiate joy. These joyful thoughts if used regularly will fill your living experience with events that make you radiate joy. The key to living a happy life is thinking it first.

MESSAGE 335

Read the following words out loud and speak them with emotion to bring the best result.

"I radiate health, joy, and positivity. I bring good to the world, and good comes back to me. I am overflowed with great synchronicities and positive interactions. I am surrounded by people who love me. My life is filled with positive people and circumstances. As I see good, I do good, and so I receive. I am abundant, and prosperous in many ways. I full of energy, good will, and well-being. And so it is and will be."

MESSAGE 336

Repeat the following words out loud as it will help us relieve you from any negative blockages and fears.

"I release all fears that are blocking me from moving forward in my life. I intentionally ask that those fears, blockages, guilt or hatred from my past, or from any other life that follows me around, be released into the light and be disintegrated now.

To the people that have wrong me, I release the wrong done to me so that I revive. To the people I have wronged I ask forgiveness and pray for utter wellbeing and bliss to them and me.

To all sickness, sadness or pain be released from my physical body so that I am renewed once again. Be released into the light so that my energy is vibrant, healthy and intact.

So it is."

MESSAGE 337

Money on their own is empty, pointless. You should not lust for money but pray for the emotion of what money will buy.

Instead of wishing for money to purchase a new car, ponder upon the joy that new car will bring, ask that the cosmos brings you the means to have that emotion. Talk to the cosmos as that always hears, why do you need the car? What would it bring? How would it make your life better? How will it help others?

This is not to justify your desire, but to find the energy of the desire so that it finds you.

MESSAGE 338

Music brings peace, if you focus on its rhythm, you find stillness.

MESSAGE 339

Don't try too hard to connect with us as we are always a call away. There is no special action to take or ritual to follow. All you have to do is direct your attention towards us, and we will be there.

MESSAGE 340

There is joy in every moment. As you pause time, you can savor it.

Stop time right now: remove thought and notice all that exists. If you taste food, put your focus on the flavor, if you hear a bird song, notice its great melody, if you talk to someone you love, feel the emotion. All you live is magnificent, if you could stop time often, you won't miss it.

MESSAGE 341

The answer lies all around you. Did you notice the synchronicities? The repetitions? They bring you answers.

MESSAGE 342

Enjoy every moment. Close your eyes and listen. Breathe. Feel.

As you do this you re-center, you clear your mind. You can find inner peace and guidance.

MESSAGE 343

Nothing is impossible, your thought, desire, and positivity bring you all that wish for.

MESSAGE 344

People do not come into your life randomly. They are there to move you forward, teach you lessons and help you find your path. When those people have concluded their purpose, then they move on.

Some might not be there to stay, but that does not mean that their presence was in vain.

MESSAGE 345

When you do good, do it for the feeling it brings. It is consolidation, oneness.

MESSAGE 346

A child has great ideas, constant inspiration, and positive energy. Why do you think is that?

Their mind is not concerned with thoughts, troubles, and worries. As they are free, they experience joy, as joy presides so does inspiration and great ideas.

Take a lesson from them.

MESSAGE 347

Let things come as they do. Do not try to alter the events, or force a solution. What you can do is direct them find a great outcome, by believing ALL WILL IS AND WILL WELL.

MESSAGE 348

Congratulations on coming this far. Think back to all that you have achieved along the way.

You are now wiser, stronger and more aware. Your life turns a shift for the best, and we are with you.

MESSAGE 349

No matter where you stand, no matter if you perceive your state of life difficult or carefree, you are always being moved towards greatness. Don't forget this.

MESSAGE 350

What if it doesn't happen yet? What if some believe it is impossible or very difficult. If you believe it, then the universe is by your side, and so are we. Then, the odds are in your favor.

MESSAGE 351

Change should not be feared but embraced. You cannot grow from being still, you grow by moving forward. Only then you gain things you didn't have before.

MESSAGE 352

Be thankful; feel appreciation as this is the language of the cosmos. It hears you say "yes, I want more of this great emotion."

MESSAGE 353

Do not be jealous of what another has. Do not think they don't deserve their success. You are a judge of your own life, and you control it from the inside. Jealousy darkens positive outcome. They have taken control of their inner world, and so can you.

MESSAGE 354

Your thought is your driving wheel. Your life is the car.

We know you like symbolism, we couldn't find a better one.

MESSAGE 355

Your natural state of being is joy, purity, and well-being. You were born in that state. Thoughts fear and ego overshadow this state, but it can easily be dominant once again.

MESSAGE 356

"Archangel Michael" you can call, and we shall appear by tuning into your essence. "Protect me" you can direct, and be certain we shall stand guards and face your fears.

MESSAGE 357

If you get an impulse, act upon it. We direct you.

MESSAGE 358

Remember that you are entitled to enjoy the luxuries, the abundance, the riches of this planet.

They are there for you.

MESSAGE 359

Love all that you are, and embrace all your differences. You are created perfect, we see you as such. When you see it too, you will be on your way to greatness.

MESSAGE 360

You are on your way for great gifts and showers of abundance. Spread your arms wide and invite them in.

MESSAGE 361

Expect the practicality of projects to come forth that transform the planet. There is a shift in your political system, your economic system, your social system. Expect harmony in terms of race relationships, gender relationships, age relationships, national relationships. Your world is transforming into all you have been yearning for. As the world changes, so are you.

MESSAGE 362

Do not rely on other people's judgment. Their perceptions are different as they have a different life's path. What they might see as bad, you might perceive as good. The way you see the world is unique, don't let another lead the way.

MESSAGE 363

If support is all you need to move ahead, then we give you plenty. Ask us to show you our support, and you will perceive it in many, many ways.

We support you.

MESSAGE 364

The stars shine bright, but not everyone notices them every night. They are always bright, however.

If you stand in the city, you cannot see their shine. As you step away to solitude, you see their glory. Sometimes stepping away from the crowd is all you need to shine brightly.

MESSAGE 365

We love you and surround you, always.

NOTE FROM THE AUTHOR:

Did you enjoy this book? If so, will you help the Angel's journey "Awaken" more people? Leave your amazing review on http://www.amazon.com/

It would really matter to me.

As a spiritual teacher, I collect recollections and experiences from spiritual practitioners to expand my expertise and put together in a future project. If you want to share your tips and experiences email me at amelia@ameliabert.com

Sign up to my exclusive newsletter and get an instant 20% discount and gain access to free bonus materials, enlightening articles, and stay updated on future projects.

You can sign up here:
http://ameliabert.com/

And follow me on social media:

https://www.facebook.com/theAngelbook/

https://twitter.com/Author_AmeliaB

https://www.linkedin.com/in/ameliabert

As a gift to you that you have made it his far, I give you a free EBook on Number Sequences, because even numbers bring you messages from spirit. *http://amzn.to/29kbVGt*

Many blessings to you.

FROM THIS AUTHOR:

THE TRUTH OF ALL THAT IS

In this book, the Angels respond to all your inquiries, thoughts and prayers. They share their wisdom, enlighten and empower. There are lessons to be learned, benefits to be gained, assistance to be given, truth to be revealed. They talk to you directly, if you would only allow the words to move through you, you will succeed your own personal transformation.

NUMBER SEQUENCES & THEIR MESSAGES

Do you get a glimpse of repetitive numbers? Do you notice number sequences like 1111, 222, 44 often?

They are not random; they bring you messages. They are Angel Numbers, and in this booklet, you will learn all about them. Unravel them; discover their Divine Guidance.

INSIDE YOU WILL DISCOVER:

When numbers bring messages, What do they mean; How to work with numbers to get answers to your questions.

THE GUIDEBOOK TO YOUR INNER POWER

This book presents spiritual practices in a step by step process to help you unleash your inner potential. Discover explanations, techniques and secrets in a broad how-to guide for all.

Explore your spiritual side, get in touch with your Divinity, unlock your power.

GET THEM NOW IN ALL ONLINE BOOKSTORES!
And from this website: http://ameliabert.com/

EMPOWERING MEDITATION:

Invoking cosmic energy & Divine Light

This is not your usual guided meditations; they are channeled with the Angels.
Amelia Bert as an Angel Intuitive, translates the Angel words into these meditations that provide high energy and empowerment.
Experience their Divine Energy and Healing Light.

Find it in Mp3 and CD and Online Streaming.

GET ANSWERS FROM THE ANGELS

Do you want to connect with Amelia and the Angels to get direct assistance on your path, and answers to your questions?

Amelia is currently offering intuitive readings with your Guardian Angels and Spirit Guides. All you have to do is reach out.

We help you with an exclusive one time discount of 20% for any intuitive readings in the website:

http://bit.ly/1LGvTTT

Your answers are only a few clicks away.

Amelia Bert

OWN UNIQUE HIGH ENERGY ARTWORK

Hurry to get the original painting pieces of Amelia Bert. Those spiritual paintings were created with Angel inspiration and contain high energy that empowers the space and people of their environment.

There are limited paintings, original and signed by Amelia Bert. Order and get your with free shipping worldwide!

http://bit.ly/1T7N3lz

ABOUT THE AUTHOR:

Amelia Bert is a freelance author and online journalist. At twenty five, she discovered her intuitive side, and mastered the clairaudient and clairvoyant ability to connect with spirit. She chooses to solely communicate with lighted spirits such as Angels that guide and inspire her.

She works closely with the Angels, through her psychic abilities. She gathers wisdom and information in that way, and shares it through her books and meditations. She aims to help others make a connection with their higher consciousness and discover their life's purpose.

Amelia has a degree in English language and literature. She spends her time writing, learning from the Angels, and painting. She lives with her fiancée and three cats and she plans to travel the world.

She wants to hear from you! Don't be shy, connect with her here: amelia@ameliabert.com

ACKNOWLEDMGENTS

Several vectors and beautiful sketches in this book are designed by Freepik. The front cover is created by Freepik, P.I and K.H

Thank you all.

Special appreciation to all my Angels, spiritual guides and spiritual teachers that join me every time I ask for support and assist with the creation of this and all my books.

Thank all of you for reading and supporting me. Being a young author is not easy, I have been rejected many times by editors and agents until I have built up the courage to start on my own. Now I am thankful I did. You have supported me through every post and every book. With your support I keep going to help spread spiritual knowledge and the Angels' love.

I love you.

Amelia

94147440R00222

Made in the USA
Columbia, SC
19 April 2018